Adaptive Resistance Training

The Ultimate Transformation Programme.

RUSSELL CLARK

Contents

INTRODUCTION 5
ABOUT THE AUTHOR 6
MY STORY 7
THE ADAPTIVE RESISTANCE TRAINING SYSTEM 17
    Training with Weights 18
    Training frequency 21
    How much weight should be used? 22
    How many Reps should be done? 23
    The Repetition Range 24
    How to Progress 25
    A Secret 26
    Back to Basics - a Reminder 27
    The One Rep Max 28
    Recording your Findings 29
    Tracking your Development 31
    Body-Part Measuring 32
    Body-Measurement Table 33
    1RM, 80% and Rep range Recording Table 35
    Week 1 Basic Routine 36
    Week 2 Basic Routine 37
    Week 3 Leg Routine 38
    Week 4 Calves Routine 39
    Week 5 Shoulder Routine 40
    Week 6 Back Routine 41

Week 7 Chest Routine 42

Week 8 Arms Routine 43

Week 9 Abdominal Routine 44

Week 10 Basic Routine 45

Example - Completed Workout Sheet 46

A FINAL WORD 48

FUTHER READING 49

QUESTIONS AND ANSWERS 50

Adaptive Resistance Training

INTRODUCTION

This programme is designed for both men and women, young or older. It is for those who want to prepare themselves, before joining a gym as well as for those who have been going to the gym for a while and find that they have not made any progress at all or they have reached a plateau in their training. It is for those who may be finding it hard to see the *'wood for the trees'*; getting bogged down in all the different routines and confused with all the contradictory information and advice. It is for those who have a reason for wanting to go to the gym - a goal to work towards. For those who want to achieve their objectives in the shortest possible time. For those who want to know that what they are doing is working. And for those who don't want to waste any more time. It is for those who want a simple, concise scientifically, tried and tested method of training to promote muscular growth, improve cardio-vascular fitness and increase general well-being.

The trainee, you will find this Adaptive Resistance Training (ART) system enjoyable and highly motivational. You will find your general appearance improve, your strength increase and your overall fitness sky-rocket. Friends and family may comment, within weeks of starting this programme, on how well you are looking.

The specific exercises outlined in this book are not described in detail. The reader, therefore, is recommended to search the Internet for examples of the exercises or consult their local gymnasium or contact the author if in there is any doubt relating to an exercise name or how to perform an exercise.

The author will not be held responsible for anyone who, as a result of using information from this writing suffers injury or ill health. Advice from your doctor should be sought before using any information in this book, which may affect your health.

ABOUT THE AUTHOR

Russell Clark is a lifetime natural bodybuilder with nearly 40 years of experience. He is a qualified teacher (CertEd) and certified practitioner of Neuro-Linguistics (NLP). He has been a personal development coach for over 20 years - helping clients achieve their maximum potential in health and fitness, as well as helping them improve their quality of life.

Russell combines his knowledge of health and fitness with that of NLP to provide a service to individuals wishing to improve their quality of life. He has worked with bodybuilding competitors, both male, and female, as well as offering instructional packages for personal trainers who want to provide the ART programme to their clients.

Russell provides a unique service for his clients. His mission, through education, guidance, and support, is to improve the lives of others.

MY STORY

I suppose all this bodybuilding and fitness craze, for me, started in 1978 when I was serving in the Royal Navy. The ship, HMS Diomede, was tied up alongside in Portsmouth for the Christmas period. I had drawn the short-straw and had the unenviable task of remaining on duty throughout the Christmas period whilst two-thirds of the crew had home-leave. I didn't mind, though, as it was really quiet and relaxed - a unique experience on board what was usually is a very noisy and busy Leander class frigate.

One day, as the weather was good, I went on to the jetty to clean my Yamaha RD250 motorcycle. It was great in those days as you could ride a powerful motorcycle on 'L' (learner) plates. After giving it a good wash and polish I decided to take it for a spin to the end of the jetty and back. It was only a couple of hundred yards, or so, there and back. What happened next was relayed to me by a police officer, upon my awakening in the Royal Portsmouth Hospital. I was told that I had been involved in a head-on collision with an oncoming car and that it was my fault. The thing was that I could not remember anything that happened so I just had to take the word of the police officer. I had been on the wrong side of the jetty and hit the front of a Vauxhall Victor as it traveled towards me. I was shown photographs of the mangled wreckage and was told that I was lucky to be alive. The car was a write-off and my bike didn't look in peak condition either, to say the least. The doctors told me that it appeared that I survive the accident because I didn't see it happen. They went on to say that if I had seen the accident I would have stiffened up my body on impact, as I flew over the handlebars of my bike and the roof of the car, covering several hundred feet, then hitting a large yellow rubbish skip, head-first, I would have no doubt suffered far greater injuries, or even death. As it was I had only sustained a fractured left arm and a few scratches and bruises.. Oh, and I forgot to mention that I wasn't wearing a crash helmet, either. It was the dockyard, after all, not a public road. A lesson learned there!

After a few days in the hospital, I was discharged. Being unable to carry out my duties over the Christmas period I was sent home, on sick leave, where I spend Christmas at my parents house, arm in a sling and wondering how this accident happened. To this day I still don't know.

Anyway, after a few weeks of recovery, I was back in Portsmouth, visiting the doctor. He told me that if I was to have any chance of being fit for duty, in time for the ship sailing, and to reduce risk of receiving the higher than normal inevitable fine for not being fit for active duty, I should look at doing some form of resistance training, to bring my left arm up to strength. So taking his advice I did a bit of research and I bought a Bullworker exerciser. The Bullworker was marketed on the fact that its design and development was founded on isometric exercise, which was one of the fastest and safest techniques for building stronger muscles. Well, I was sold on that. This was my first experience of any form of training for muscular strength and believe it or not, it worked. With a few weeks, the strength in my left arm had increased enough, so much so that I was passed as fit for duty and I was able to join my ship again in time for its sailing.

As I continued to use the Bullworker, over the preceding months, my muscles started to develop more. I also became aware that others had taken this muscle building to a level whereby they were entering competitions. There was a guy called Arnold Schwarzenegger and others like a guy who had won a competition that was called the Mr. Olympia, Frank Zane. Whilst Arnold was a big guy, Frank Zane looked slimmer and I could relate to him more. There was hope for me, I thought.

I had not excelled at sport at school. In fact, despite my determination to be good at something and to be accepted as part of a team sport, I was always the one to be picked last for a team or the one who stood on the sidelines for the duration of the event, as a substitute. I was, however, picked by my peers to play in goals in winter, during the lunch breaks. Not real goals, though. The ones marked out on the ground with a couple of school blazers. But goals, never-the-less. I was chosen to be in goals only because no one else was prepared to roll about in the mud or hit the hard ice on those freezing days when that low shot came hurtling towards the goal. But the motivation behind the choices others made relating to me being included in the team was not important to me. I was always enthusiastic and willing. In the summer, however, everyone wanted to be a goalie and I was, disappointedly, banished to the side-lines as an onlooking, envious, spectator until the winter winds returned, when again I would get my chance to shine (in my small way).

Being short in height and slight in build, there weren't many sports I seemed to be good at. And my peers thought that too. No long legs for running, or long arms for throwing. No weight on me to throw about on the rugby field, no size or bulk to be intimidating and I wasn't tall enough to play in those full-sized goals. On the few occasions, I did get the chance to play in full-sized goals, due to the absence of the first-choice goalkeeper, the opposition soon realised that if they kicked the ball high enough I couldn't reach it. So they just kept kicking those balls over me, from near or even far. It didn't matter, I was not ever going to stop them. However, in a sports hall, five-a-side was another thing. The goal crossbar was even lower than my height. No one could get a ball past me there. That is where I did find my niche. I have to smile, looking back at those times. But what future was there at being a five-a-side goalie?

But hold on a minute, what about this muscle building thing that I had just discovered as a result of my accident? Now here was something that I could do, which did not need anyone's permission or acceptance. The bonus here was I didn't have to wait for anyone else to let me join in. There was no exclusive club. It was just me. So I started lifting weights and I was hooked.

As time went on, with a thirst for knowledge and in an attempt to educate myself on the subject of building muscles, I searched for anything that would help me build my body. At the time there seemed only to be the muscle magazines, which were perched high up on the top shelves of the main newsagents, right next to some questionable magazines showing scantily dressed ladies on the covers. For someone who, at the time, was 5 foot 4" tall and a reserved lad of 17 years of age, it was no mean feat, both physically and mentally to muster up the courage, to stretch further than I comfortably could, to grab hold of a magazine from the infamous, top-shelf. Then to take it to the checkout and pay for it, wondering if the lady behind the desk thought me a bit odd for buying a magazine which showed men with very little covering their bodies. When asked if I wanted a bag for it, I unequivocally said yes, as I didn't want anyone else to see what I had bought. There were even times when it was too busy in the newsagent, I couldn't even bring myself to buy a magazine. I was very conscious of what others thought about me in those days and what I assumed they thought about men, muscles, and men looking at men with muscles if you get my meaning. So I chose my times to get the magazines when there were fewer customers. But I did get them and I was inspired by the images I saw.

A year later I came to the end of my draft on HMS Diomede and was assigned to HMS Fife. This was a shore-based posting for a year as the ship was in for a major refit and inhabitable. My residence was the shore base, HMS Nelson. This was an opportunity for me to join a gym. There was only one I knew of, in Portsmouth. That was the City Gym. I joined the almost straight away.

As a sailor, I wasn't exactly made welcome by the gym locals. I think the owner only warmed to me after about three months of me attending. But it was ok because I didn't need approval, support or acceptance. It was all down to me. I went to the gym day in - day out. Sometimes six times a week. It was a crazy time. I was of the mind that I had to train hard and often. I tried out all the different exercises, with little care or notice of if they benefitted me. It was not even a trial and error exercise. I was just following the routines, outlined in the magazines. They worked for the big guys so they must work. Right? A year soon went by and then I was assigned to HMS Hermes for the rest of my service. Being an aircraft carrier, the Hermes had lots of space and more weights available than I had been used to on the smaller ships. The ship was more stable on the sea, so the weights would not roll about. I remember trying to train on the Diomede and having to wait for the ship to settle before I could a set of chest press. On the Hermes, I could train in just about any sea condition. The ship didn't even seem like it was moving. In late 1981 we even went through a hurricane, on our way to Florida, losing a Land Rover, which was chained down, off the upper deck and we didn't even notice the rough sea. That's how stable the ship was. I would train daily to the sound of the music from the film 'Rocky', still following those routines that I read about in the magazines. I was still not making any real gains. But who cared! Not me, I was enjoying myself.

In 1982, on returning from my last tour of duty, I was reassigned to the shore base, HMS Nelson where I ended my service. Then I was back into civi-street, back home and on to find a new gym to train in.

I soon found employment, working sixty hours a week, in a factory. There was a gym I passed on the way to work, that was called Brian Taylor's. It was above a pub called The Drum. Brian Taylor was somewhat of a celebrity in Doncaster. He was a former Mr. Yorkshire, Mr. North East Britain and he came 6th in the NABBA Amateur Mr. Universe contest in 1976. I never got to meet Brian as he died of a heart attack in 1980, at the age of 38. But the gym was still thriving, in the hands of his wife Edna.

The Drum (the name of the pub), as it was known because it was easier to explain to people where the gym was located, was where any up and coming bodybuilder would train. So I joined the gym and I soon got into the same routine as everyone else there, doing the split routines that were so much the norm in those days. Chest, back, biceps on Monday. Shoulders, legs, and triceps on Wed and then back around again on Friday. Week in - week out. Multiple sets and at least two hours in the gym, for each session, if not longer. Training before work, when on twelve-hour nights or after work when on the twelve-hour day shift. Gee, it was hard. But I was young and crazy.

In 1983, after a year of training at the gym, I was encouraged to compete in my first bodybuilding competition. It was the local Mr. Doncaster - the competition that nearly everyone in the gym entered and wanted to win. It was an annual event. All the training and preparation led to this one competition each year. I can't remember anyone who didn't train at Brian Taylor's winning the Mr. Doncaster. It just could not be conceived. Needless to say, that year I didn't win or get anywhere close, but suffice to say that the top three places went to members of Brian Taylor's gym. If there was one thing I learned from training at The Drum was what it took a great deal of self-discipline to train and compete. The training advice I was given by seasoned gym-goers was not backed up with evidence. But everyone trained the same and reached their potential given the same training beliefs and conditions. So what did it matter that we were all training wrong?

Still armed with the periodicals, a few books on the subject of training and diet, and another year under my belt, I was determined to give Mr. Doncaster a go the following year. Again not placing in the contest.

Yet again 1985, 1986 and 1987 went by, to no avail. It was so frustrating to think that despite all the books and magazine articles that I had read, inwardly digested and applied to my training, I still couldn't get myself to the standard required to win, even a local bodybuilding contest. What to do?

Then, by chance, after the Mr. Doncaster contest in 1987, I came upon a different method of training. This was something called High-Intensity Training. It was completely different from the training everyone else was doing, or anything I had done. It seemed to have scientific evidence showing that it worked, which was something refreshing. There were no split routines, no training every day of the week, no doing multiple sets. There was less training time required and boasted better results. I needed to research this more. I was intrigued and started reading the works of Arthur Jones, the inventor of Nautilus and pioneer of High-Intensity Training and I discovered the training routines of Mike Mentzer, who had adopted the High-Intensity philosophy.

Very quickly I liked what I found and decided to try this method of training to see if it worked, for me. I collected enough information to enable me to design a HIT programme and put it in to practice. I had nothing to lose. I took measurements of all my body parts and worked out what I needed to do.

After just ten weeks I could not believe the difference it made to my physique. I had felt and seen my physique change for the better gradually over the ten weeks but it wasn't until I did the final assessment that it confirmed to me that this type of training worked.

I had developed my physique more in those ten weeks than I had done in the previous eight or so years. This was crazy. I was getting positive feedback from other members of the gym. Even though I told them about the training I was doing and indeed, they saw me training in the gym, they still didn't believe it worked.

Russell gets title at last

continued with another ten-week cycle, followed by another. Then after just under one year of training the HIT way I was ready to enter the Mr. Doncaster contest again. This time, though, I won. I also won the Class 3 (5' 6" and under) Open Central Britain, which was on the same day at the same show. As a result, I was invited to enter the Class 3 Novice Britain Final, later on in the year. And I won that too, although there was only two of us in the class.

All those waisted years. All the money spent on magazines and books which served only to confuse me and keep me wanting to find out new methods which were written about in more magazines and books, that I would have to buy. Now, who's the mug?

But I had the foresight to be different and find the answer to how to stimulate muscular grown and achieve maximum potential in the shortest possible time. I had found the training philosophy that no one wanted us to know about. Some are making money out of the inquisitive, aspiring bodybuilder. Those, should I say, apart from Arthur Jones et al. The information on how to train properly was available all along, just brushed under the carpet. But Arthur Jones was making waves and ruffling some feathers. Now, so was I.

From the time I discovered HIT, in 1987, I have trained using the High-Intensity methodology. Since that time I have continued to adapt and evolve, developing my own ten-week weight training programme, which I now call Adaptive Resistance Training.

Fast forward to 2024, at the age of 63, I am still using my ART system of training. I have competed many times since winning Mr. Doncaster, in 1988. Sometimes having 5 - 6 years away from competition. But despite this, I have always come back even better than before. In 2018, after 6 years away, I placed 2nd in the over 50 Natural Mr. Yorkshire and 3rd at the Britain Finals. Then in 2019 I, again, placed 2nd in the Yorkshire and qualified for the European Championships where I placed 5th and then in October 2019 I achieved 4th in the Britain Finals. My fiancée, Karen, entered her first Figure contest, at the age of 54, in 2018, winning a 'Best Transformation' award and in 2019 she placed 3rd in the Over 40s Toned Figure Class, qualifying for the British Finals with me, where she also placed 4th. She had only been training since 2016 but still was able to stand along-side seasoned trainers as an equal.

And, bringing us right up-to-date, I won the Over 60s Natural Mr. Britain in 2022. Karen and I put our achievements down to the HIT training philosophy.

So to sum up, my ART system is a methodology of training, using short duration, high-intensity resistance weight training is designed specifically to maximise healthy, natural physical development. It is based on the HIT principals of Arthur Jones et al.

- It allows for the formulation of the ideal weight and repetitions to be used, specific to the individual's skeletal and muscular structure.
- It encourages adaptation of exercises and flexibility in the frequency of training to minimise any incidence of injury and to also promote muscle growth, through proper exercise, rest and recuperation.
- It helps the individual reach their full potential, based on their specific genetic capabilities, within the shortest possible time.

So this training is for males and females of any sporting discipline who want to tone and build muscle, improve cardiovascular fitness and promote fat loss.

Adaptive Resistance Training

Over 60s
Natural Mr Britain

THE ADAPTIVE RESISTANCE TRAINING SYSTEM

Training with Weights

There are numerous weight training routines available and written about in magazines and books. All claim having contributed to making a related bodybuilder the person he is today. They have evolved over the years and, in the main, they have been designed to sell magazines to keep the reader/trainer motivated. Little attention is given to how and why a particular weight training routine would work and in the absence of such an explanation the reader/trainer has no other option than to set about a process of trial and error.

Any form of resistance training will indeed stimulate muscle growth. So too would picking up, after others, the weights from the gym floor and replacing them on the racks. However, once the new trainer's muscles have adapted, no more growth would take place.

Year in - year out, the trainer seems to be oblivious to the fact that progress is slow or even non-existent. Enthusiastically (s)he grabs for the latest magazine or book to find a new routine that could help stimulate growth. But, yet again, after another few months, to no avail. And the search goes on, year-in-year-out.

There is, however, but one training philosophy that has been scientifically proven to promote muscular development. This philosophy, developed, endorsed and promoted by the innovator Arthur Jones and adopted by Mike Mentzer et al, is the High-Intensity Training (HIT) methodology.

This booklet, at the time of writing, does not contain the scientific theory to substantiate the positive claims of the HIT methodology. To do so would make the book too long and possibly detract from what the reader primarily wants to achieve, that being to get into the gym and stimulate muscle growth.

However, suffice to say, now that one is fully aware that a training methodology exists and works, you would be right to believe that one would be foolish not to embrace it.

The trainer is encouraged to seek out further material on the subject of High-intensity training, to increase awareness. There is information available on the internet and in many books. I have included a reference to further reading at the end of this book.

The following sections, in this booklet, outline the fundamental elements associated with the high-intensity training methodology. Read each one in turn and only move on when you have fully understood the essence of each heading.

The booklet also provides you with all the information you need to promote muscular development, tone up and trim down, with step-by-step instructions for assessment and training. You will not need any other information - everything you need from start to finish is here in this booklet.

Adaptive Resistance Training

Let's get Started

Training frequency

Ideally, we should be able to train every day of the week with no ill effect and see gradual muscular development. However, in reality, the muscle will respond more if an intelligent approach is adopted which facilitates time for recovery and growth.

In essence the muscles, therefore, need to be subjected to an amount of force greater than that which it can comfortably handle, to encourage growth. Once this has been achieved the muscle, then, must be given time to repair.

There are no hard and fast guidelines to say how long one should allow for recovery. This depends on genetics, age, and nutrition. But one can start by using a basic premise that the muscle would need a minimum of 48 hours and a maximum of 72 hours before subjecting it to further resistance training.

Subjecting the muscle to a further onslaught, before it has had time to recover would thwart growth and encourage the incidence of injury. We shall, therefore, commit to giving the muscles a day of rest between training, thus training three times a week - for example, Monday, Wednesday and Friday or Tuesday, Thursday and Saturday.

How much weight should be used?

The load that each muscle can handle, for a specific exercise is determined by choosing a weight, which one can only lift for one repetition. This weight is known as the 'One Rep Maximum' (1RM).

For example: in determining the one rep' maximum (1RM) of a barbell bicep curl, one should select a barbell which has a weight that it is believed the trainer can only lift for a single rep'. And in strict and definite form, carry out a single rep'. When this rep' is complete, without putting the weight down or pausing for an unnecessary length of time, one should attempt a second rep'. If a second rep' is achieved then one can deduce that the weight was not sufficiently heavy for the muscle to fail at the first rep'. At this point, the barbell should be put down. A rest of 5 minutes should be concluded before carrying out the process again, only this time with a slightly heavier weight. This process should be carried out until no more than one rep' can be achieved. This weight will then be known as the 1RM. One should, realistically, estimate the weight to be used at the first attempt, as it should be born in mind that the muscle will weaken with the advent of an unnecessary number of attempts, giving a false result.

If this process is carried out with all exercises, one will then know the 1RM for any given exercise.

This practice should be applied to every different exercise. However, there are some exercises where it would be dangerous to determine the 1RM by this method. For example, squats. For this exercise and others, where it may be unrealistic to apply the principal method, a mathematical formula can be used as explained further in this book.

How many Reps should be done?

Once the 1RM weight has been determined, a set comprising of several reps should be performed using 80% of the 1RM. For example, 80% of a 1RM of 100lbs would be 80lbs. The set should be done in strict form, taking four seconds to do the concentric and eccentric movements (lifting and lowering), until no more reps can be done - achieving momentarily muscular failure.

Each different exercise will see a varying number of repetitions achieved. Whist, for example, one may achieve 8 reps on, say, the barbell bicep curl, one may achieve 15 reps on the squats. This is not uncommon. In fact, it would question the validity of the principle of ascertaining the 1RM, if all exercises gleaned the same number of repetitions.

It has also been identified through studies, that the lower body parts require more reps than the upper body-parts. So to achieve 15-20 reps with 80% of the ORM would be common place.

The Repetition Range

After finding the number of reps, which can be done by each different muscle and each different exercise, we then need to find a range within which we can work. We just deduct 1 rep and add 1 rep to the number of reps achieved with our 80% weight. Ie: if 8 reps were achieved by using 80% of the 1RM, then by taking 1 rep away and also adding 1 rep to the 8 reps would give a range of 7 to 9.

So now one has been able to determine the 1RM of a given exercise, worked out the weight to be used for a set and determined a range within which to work. For example: Barbell Curl: 1RM = 100lbs, 80% of 100lbs = 80lbs, 8 reps done 80lbs gives a range of 7 to 9 reps.

How to Progress

The muscle-building process is progressive. The pre-determined weight that one uses to subject the muscle to the right amount of force to encourage growth will have to be increased at some stage, as the muscle adapts to the weight being used. This increase in weight should be done when one more rep is achieved above the upper limit of the predetermined range. I.e.: if the range is 7 to 9 reps and 10 reps are achieved then the weight used should be increased. The increase in weight should not be too much, preventing the trainer from achieving, at the very least, the lower limit of the set range, but it must be enough to stimulate muscle growth further.

Suffice to say that one should make sure that this achievement is consistent before increasing the weight. The test for this would be to achieve this 'one rep over the upper limit' on 2 or 3 further occasions. Once one is satisfied that the upper range marker has been sufficiently breached then one should increase the weight by 5% and round it to the nearest 5lbs or equivalent. When the weight has been increased one would expect, on the next training session, the reps to drop back down to within the range but not below the lower limit. If the reps fall below the lower range limit, the weight is too heavy and, therefore, should be reduced. It should, however, be on very rare occasions that this occurs, as the increase in weight is just enough to allow the muscle to adapt and not too much to prevent it from achieving the number of reps that fall within the pre-determined range.

A Secret

I have advised a lot of people in the past but there is one factor, which has seen the downfall of every good intention, this is that a written routine had not been used. It takes a lot of will-power to stick to a training routine at the best of times, but to stick to one without it being in writing is near on impossible. I have always encouraged the formulation of the routines before the day of the workout. If possible the next work-out routine should be done as near to the completion of the preceding routine, when the experience of the work-out is still fresh in one's mind.

It may sound strange that above all other things relating to weight training this is the key to succeeding. But the advantage of utilising a written log is that, whilst training, one does not have to think about the number of reps or the weight needed to be used nor the combination or sequence of the routine. This releases the mind so that one can concentrate on performing the exercise properly. Additionally, you will never go to the gym and wonder what it is you should be doing or coming away wondering if you have done enough.

This book, therefore, contains the tables with which contain the weekly routines and provide a medium with which one will A: know exactly what exercises you should be doing in any given workout, B: allow you to record the weight used and reps achieved so you can track your progress and C: plan your next workout in advance.

Back to Basics - a Reminder

One failure of most is to misunderstand the basic training fundamentals and incorporate time-consuming and energy-wasting exercises, which do nothing but hinder the progress of muscular development. Much more can be achieved by keeping to the basic exercises, which work the main muscle groups. The basic muscle groups are Chest, Back, Legs, Shoulders, Triceps, Biceps, and Calves. The basic exercises are Bench Press, Lat Pull-down, Squat, Shoulder Press, Triceps Pushdowns, Biceps Curl, and Calf Raise.

Additionally, one should not wander from the fundamental principals of this HIT regime, as to do so would reduce its effectiveness and hinder ones muscular development.

The One Rep Max

Where it may be unrealistic to apply the principal method, to determine the 1RM, a mathematical formula can be used. The type of exercises where this would apply would be Squats and Dead-lift. There may be other exercises that may necessitate the application of this formula, because of the type of equipment that may or may not be available. Common sense should be applied to ascertain the appropriate method of assessing your 1RM.

To find out your one-rep max (1RM), carry out a set with a weight that you feel comfortable with until no more reps can be achieved. Record the number of repetitions and divide this number by 30 and then add 1. Then multiply the result by the weight you lifted. For example:

The formula

- 1RM = ((# reps divided by 30)+1) x weight;
- An Example
- 8 reps have been achieved with a weight of 100lbs
- Therefore:
- (8 reps divided by 30)+1) x 100lbs = 126lbs
- 8 divided by 30 = .266, .266+1=1.266, 1.266 x 100=126.66. 127 (rounded) is the 1RM.

It may be true that the 1RM, for all exercises, could be determined by applying this mathematical formula. However, one should be confident in the results by sitting side by side those results of the principal method, to check any variation, where possible.

Recording your Findings

To assist you in recording your results, a table has been provided for you in the next section of this booklet. All the basic exercises have been listed, with space to add other exercises as felt necessary, when a new exercise presents itself over throughout the ten-week programme.

The table allows for the recording of both the formulated method as well as the standard method of determining the 1RM.

The 1RM should be recorded in the first column. The 80% of the 1RM in the second column and, when a set is done with this 80% weight, the number of reps achieved, recorded in the third column. The range will then be worked out by deducting 1 rep and adding 1 rep to the number of reps one achieved with the 80% of the 1RM.

- Example 1 - standard method:
- Weight lifted 80lbs for 12 reps.

	Weight (a)	Reps (b)	1 Rep Max (c)	80% 1 Rep Max (d)	Reps Completed (e)	Range (f)
Thigh Ext	-	-	80lb	64lb	12	11-13

- Example 2 - formula method:
- Weight lifted 150lb for 12 reps. (12 divided by 30)+1 (multiplied by 150=210)

	Weight (a)	Reps (b)	1 Rep Max (c)	80% 1 Rep Max (d)	Reps Completed (e)	Range (f)
Squats	150lb	12	210lb	170lb	-	13-15

Adaptive Resistance Training

Working it out

Tracking your Development

It would be recommended that one make a record, photographic and the body-part measurements, before the commencement of this ten-week programme and after its completion, so that it can be ascertained just how much progress one has made on this programme.

Additionally, from time-to-time one may find an ebb in one's motivation. This is not uncommon. The mind is an area that must be controlled and there are various methods and techniques that one can use to maintain one's motivation. I would encourage anyone to read the psychological writings relating to personal achievement, so to obtain a better understanding of how one can achieve one's goal through thought control.

If you are looking at achieving your goals in the shortest possible time, there is one thing you should know. For hundreds of years, successful men have known the secret to achievement. Written by Napoleon Hill and other successful men, the formulae for success is: *'In order to achieve all that you desire in a given discipline, one should seek out the very person who has gone before you and learnt the strategy for success. For if you find that person and employ his knowledge, you too will achieve the same level of success, guaranteed!* '

Body-Part Measuring

NECK

Wrap the measuring tape around your neck, beginning at the Adam's apple.

CHEST

Raise your arms as your helper wraps the tape around you from back to front, crossing under your shoulders and finishing at the nipple line. Lower your arms before finalising the measurement, making sure the tape does not slip down your back. It should cross your shoulder blades behind you. Breathe fully in and record measurement. Do not pull the tape tight. Then breathe fully out and record second measurement. Add the two measurements and divide by two to achieve the average. Record this result.

UPPER ARMS

Flex and measure the largest part of each arm, at the biceps' peak.

FOREARMS

Flex the muscle by making a fist and cocking your wrist. Measure the thickest portion, up near each elbow.

WAIST

Wrap the tape around your torso, making sure it crosses over your belly button.

HIPS AND BUTTOCKS

Measure the widest point of your hips.

THIGHS

Flex your thigh. Make sure the tape goes around the largest part of each thigh. Do both legs.

CALVES

Support your weight on the opposite leg and push up on your toe with the other leg, to flex the muscle. Measure each calf at the largest point.

Body-Measurement Table

Use this table to record your measurements before commencing the ten-week programme and again after its completion. This will crystallise the progress you have made and motivate you to further your personal development.

Body Part	Before	After	Difference
Neck			
Shoulders			
Chest inhale			
Chest exhale			
Left Arm			
Right Arm			
Left Forearm			
Right Forearm			
Waist			
Hips			
Left Thigh			
Right Thigh			
Left Calf			
Right Calf			
Body Weight			
Tips	The measurements should be recorded accurately, without pulling the tape measure tight. Measurements should be taken with the muscles flexed for Arms, Forearms, Thighs and Calves. The growth you will note, after ten weeks, will be evident in the Difference Column.		

Adaptive Resistance Training

Assessment Sheets

1RM, 80% and Rep range Recording Table

This table is to be used to record your finding during your initial assessment of 1RM and ideal lower and upper rep range.

Exercise	Weight (a)	Reps (b)	1 Rep Max (c)	80% Weight (d)	Reps Done (e)	Range (f)
Thigh Ext						
Leg Curl						
Leg Press						
Calf Raise						
Pullovers						
Lat-Pulldowns						
Bench Press						
Side Lat-Raise						
Shoulder Press						
Seated Row						
Tricep Pushdowns						
Bicep Curl						
Dead-Lift						

Week 1 Basic Routine

Exercise	Range	Day 1	Day 2	Day 3
Leg Extension				
Leg Curl				
Squat				
Calf Raise				
Pullovers				
Lat-Pulldowns				
Bench Press				
Side Laterals				
Seated Press				
Seated Pullins				
Tricep Pushdows				
Bicep Curl				
Stiff-legged Dead Lift				
Notes	This is the basic routine. Ensure you write the planned reps down faintly, in pencil. For example, when doing the routine, if you were aiming to achieve 8 reps for a set and achieved 8 or more then you could write it in BOLD over the faint pencil entry. (For example, 9/**45** would become **9/45**) Do not neglect the 'all-important' preparation exercises and stretching at the end of the workout. Start with a 5 minute warm-up at the beginning of every session in the form of the treadmill, stepper or stationary bike. This will warm up the legs and increase the heart-rate to a level appropriate for the training to come. At the end of the week, you may find that you are 5 - 10 percent stronger than you were when you first started.			

Week 2 Basic Routine

Exercise	Range	Day 1	Day 2	Day 3
Leg Extension				
Leg Curl				
Squat				
Calf Raise				
Pullovers				
Lat-Pulldowns				
Bench Press				
Side Laterals				
Seated Press				
Seated Pullins				
Tricep Pushdows				
Bicep Curl				
Stiff-legged Dead Lift				
Notes	This routine is the same as week one. After week one you may feel you want to up the pace a little. You will have got used to your exercises and the weights that you are using. You may have already seen jumps in strength and the amount of weight you are now using. This week you will be settling down, knowing what you are doing and able to concentrate more on the exercise, rather than the routine. Do not neglect the 'all-important' pre-warmup exercises and stretching at the end of the workout. At the end of this week, you may find that you are 5 - 10 percent stronger than you were when you first started.			

Adaptive Resistance Training

Week 3 Leg Routine

Exercise	Range	Day 1	Day 2	Day 3
Leg Press				
Thigh Extension				
Squat				
Leg Curl				
Stiff-legged Dead LiftLunges				
Lunges				
Pullovers				
Side Laterals				
Seated Press				
Bicep Curl				
Tricep Pushdows				
Chins				
Dips				
Notes	Over the coming weeks, you will specialise on different body parts. This week it is legs. It involves what is known as a double pre-exhaust. You will need to have the equipment/weights ready for the leg part of the workout because you will be going straight from one exercise to the next. The Leg Press should be followed immediately by the leg extension and then the full squat. Then the Leg Curl, immediately followed by the leg curl (approximately 10% less weight than you would normally use) and the stiff-legged dead-lift.			

Week 4 Calves Routine

Exercise	Range	Day 1	Day 2	Day 3
Calf Raise				
Leg Curl				
Calf Raise				
Leg Curl				
Pullovers				
Wide Grip Chins				
Bench Press				
Lat Pulldowns				
Lat Raise				
Shrugs				
Thigh Extension				
Leg Curl				
Squats				
Notes	The calf muscle is one used daily and one that has been subject to almost constant stress. Therefore, this muscle should be the one which can handle the most weight, pound for pound. As with every specialisation week, the exercises are grouped and should be done in quick succession. Calf raise followed quickly by leg curl. This is done twice. Put 100% effort in. The rest of the routine will work the rest of your body. Don't be upset that you may not be working a particular body part as this week they will either be rested fully or hit indirectly when doing the other exercises.			

Week 5 Shoulder Routine

Exercise	Range	Day 1	Day 2	Day 3
Pullovers				
Lateral Raise				
Shoulder Press				
Shrugs				
Upright Row				
Lateral Raise				
Shoulder Press				
Leg Press				
Calf Raise				
Calf Raise				
Bench Press				
Bicep Curl				
Tricep Pushdown				
Wrist Curl				
Reverse Wrist Curl				

Notes

This week you concentrate on shoulders.

In recent years concern has been expressed relating to the safety of doing barbell upright rows as this exercise can compromise the shoulder if done incorrectly. Therefore, I recommend using dumbbells so to allow for the natural movement of the shoulder when performing this exercise and thus reducing the risk of injury.

When doing the Lat Raise and Shoulder press for the second time, after the DB upright rows, you may find your strength dropping and you may have to reduce your second set's weights to 60% of your 1RM.

Week 6 Back Routine

Exercise	Range	Day 1	Day 2	Day 3
Pullovers				
Seated Pullins				
Wide Grip Chins				
Lat Pulldowns				
Seated Pullins				
Wide Grip Chins				
Thigh Extensions				
Leg Curl				
Leg Press				
Shoulder Press				
Stiff-Leg Deadlift				
Shrugs				
Notes	This week you will concentrate on your back. You should be giving all exercises 100% effort and have seen strength increases in all exercises, which will have transferred equally into muscle gain. This week we group exercises into 3. So Pullovers followed by seated rows, quickly followed by chins. Then Lat Pulldowns, followed by seated rows, followed by own weight, wide grip, Chins. After the first group of exercises, you may find your strength dropping and you may have to reduce your second group's weights to 60% of your 1RM.			

Week 7 Chest Routine

Exercise	Range	Day 1	Day 2	Day 3
Dumbell Flys				
Bench Press				
Dumbell Flys				
Incline Bench Press				
Dips				
Press-ups				
Thigh Extensions				
Leg Curl				
Leg Press				
Calf Raise				
Tricep Pushdowns				
Notes	This week you will do two double pre-exhaust cycles. Push your chest hard. We need to get the blood flowing into the chest muscle first by doing an activation exercise. We will do light dumbbell flys first, followed quickly with the Bench Press, then quickly followed by regular weight dumbbell flys. Then Inclined Bench, Flys and Dips again and quickly followed by press-ups. You will find you are as weak as a kitten by the press-up stage but push through and when you can't do any more regular press-ups put your knees on the floor and press out a few more reps. Remember to always go to momentarily muscular failure.			

Week 8 Arms Routine

Exercise	Range	Day 1	Day 2	Day 3
1 Rep Chin				
Barbell Curl				
1 Rep Reverse Dip				
Tricep Pushdowns				
Thigh Extension				
Leg Curl				
Shrugs				
Pullovers				
Bench Press				
Lateral Raise				
Shoulder Press				
Stiff-Leg Deadlift				
Wrist Curl				
Reverse Wrist Curl				
Notes	If you haven't done this routine before you are in for a treat. We start with a one-rep chin. With an underhand grip, we raise pull ourselves up, taking 30 seconds to get to the top and then take 30 seconds to lower. As soon as we drop from the bar we are straight into the Barbell curls, which will be about 60% of your one-rep max. Triceps are the same, doing a reverse dip.			

Week 9 Abdominal Routine

Exercise	Range	Day 1	Day 2	Day 3
Hanging Leg Raise				
Crunches				
Side Bends				
Stiff-Leg Deadlift				
Pullovers				
Chins				
Leg Extension				
Leg Curl				
Calf Raise				
Lateral Raise				
Dips				
Lat Pulldowns				
Notes	This week's routine comprises three pre-exhaust cycles. The abdominals are a muscle like all other muscle parts and as so need to be trained regularly. However, be aware that using weight on the side bends will encourage growth, resulting in a wider waist. When doing the leg raise ensure your legs are kept as straight as possible. Try not to bend at the knees. This will target the abdominals more than if you bent your knees. Penultimate week. You should have made excellent gains in both strength and size now.			

Adaptive Resistance Training

Week 10 Basic Routine

Exercise	Range	Day 1	Day 2	Day 3
Leg Extension				
Leg Curl				
Squat				
Calf Raise				
Pullovers				
Lat-Pulldowns				
Bench Press				
Side Laterals				
Seated Press				
Seated Pullins				
Tricep Pushdows				
Bicep Curl				
Stiff-legged Dead Lift				
Notes	This is your final week of your cycle. The routine is an overall body workout. Push really hard as next week you can have a rest week.			

Example - Completed Workout Sheet

Exercise	Range	Day 1	Day 2	Day 3
Leg Extension	11-13	12/55	14/55	/50
Leg Curl	6-8	5/45	7/45	/45
Squat	15-17	17/200	19/200	/210
Calf Raise	18-20	16/400	17/400	/380
Pullovers				
Lat-Pulldowns				
Bench Press				
Side Laterals				
Seated Press				
Seated Pullins				
		This example is not the full workout.		
Notes	This is an example workout sheet. The first exercise is the leg extensions. On day 1 I did 12 reps with 55lb. This was within my range so I set my target for Day 2 at 13 reps with the same weight. However, I achieved 14 reps on Day 2 so I added 5% to the 55lb and rounded it up to 58lbs and lightly pencilled in 11 reps as my target with this weight for my Day three workout. The next exercise is the Leg Curl. 6-8 being the range I set but with the weight, I worked out from the 1 rep max I only achieved 5 reps. However, not put off, I set my next workout as 6 reps with the same weight, to be sure, and achieved 7. So Day 3 is set to do the upper number of my range, 8. Squats, no problem. Within my range and going good, so increased the weight by 5% for Day 3. When I got to my calves, however, I was unable to even achieve the lower			

A FINAL WORD

You have made it. Ten weeks of training, using the ART method. You will now deserve a week off. This is a week in which the body will fully recover from the intense training you have put it through.

During your rest week, you should take your muscle measurements and your after photos. Record the results in the body measurement table and compare the before and after photos. It will be now that you will notice a difference between where you started to where you are now. You will also, from your first week to your last week's workout tables, notice an increase in strength.

During your week off, prepare your programme for another ten-week cycle.

Good luck and if you have any questions feel free to email me at
russell@studio97.co.uk

FUTHER READING

Nautilus Bulletin #1 1970 …

http://www.arthurjonesexercise.com/Bulletin1/Bulletin1.html

Nautilus Bulletin #2 1971 …

http://www.arthurjonesexercise.com/Bulletin2/Bulletin2.html

ARTHUR JONES

https://en.wikipedia.org/wiki/Arthur_Jones_(inventor)

QUESTIONS AND ANSWERS

Q. How many sets do you do on each exercise?

A. *Just one set. If you take the muscle to momentary muscular failure, one set will stimulate muscle growth.*

Q. Do I need a warm-up set?

A. *A 5-minute warm-up is recommended at the start of each session, to get the blood flowing to the legs and to elevate the heart rate, in preparation for the ART training. The cross-trainer, stepper or stationary bike will enable you to do this. However, thereafter, the system is designed so that each exercise forms as the warm-up for the next. For example, after the legs, you may be doing chest. Chest flys are designed to warm up the chest before the compound movement - bench press.*

Q. How much rest do you take between exercises?

A. *Once you start the workout, move quickly between exercises with no rest. If you have a training partner, go round one at a time. The training partner should be setting up the next exercise, whilst you are doing one. If you are on your own, group the exercises. For example - Legs: Set up Thigh Ext, Leg Curl, Squats and Calf Raise. Then go through each exercise in turn with no rest in between. Do this for the whole work-out, but make sure the setup time is quick too.*

Q. What do you do if someone is on an exercise I want?

A. *You are only doing one set. Ask them if you can jump in, whilst they rest in between sets. Say that you are only doing one set. I have never been refused.*

Q. It was really hard to hit the entire workout again, just two days later. I was sore and fatigued and I could go nowhere near the previous weights. I'm thinking to do three rest days in between workouts, what do you think?

A. *If you haven't done exercises with this intensity or you have been using weights that were below what is ideal for you, you will feel it. And yes, take an extra day or two off. It may take a few sessions for you to be able to do three days a week, in this case, but you will. The main thing here is to make sure you are fully recovered before you commence your next workout.*

Q. One question I have is: How much rest would you allow between exercises? I think you ideally don't want hardly any, but in a home gym, that's tough.

A. I can appreciate that it will be difficult, training with limited space and equipment. However, if you can group the body-part exercises and move quickly to each exercise in the group then this will be great. For example, legs: thigh ext, thigh bicep, squats. Chest: flys and pressing, Shoulders: side laterals and pressing etc. Still, however, keep the time between groups, i.e. when setting up for the next group, to a minimum. This will improve your cardiovascular fitness and ensure that the body is still warm, in preparation for the next group sets.

Q. I stared with week one, after working out my one rep max and rep range. But the squats have done downhill for some reason. What should I do?

A. Don't worry that your squats were not what you first worked out them to be. Stick with the same rep range that you will have and push above the upper limit. Once achieved increase the weight by 5% and go again in the next workout. You will get stronger and in turn your muscles will grow.

Q. Hi Russell, I've had a quick read through your book and can't get my head around doing only 1 set per exercise, 3 times a week. Then you take the set to momentary muscular failure and don't do any drops etc. This seems way too little exercise. I know Arthur Jone and Mentzer brothers championed this HIT but reading about Mike Mentzer he used multiple set training as well.

A. Yes, I can relate to what you are saying about not being able to get your head around doing only one set per exercise, three times a week. Arthur Jones was the innovator of the system and Mike Mentzer was an advocate of the methodology. Suffice to say that I can only assume that if Mike was adding sets, against the philosophy and scientifically proven methods of which Arthur Jones endorsed then it was for a specific reason, that being strength, and not necessarily for muscular hypertrophy. Give it your divided attention and commit to this routine for the ten-week period and the results will be evidence enough. Thereafter, try adding drop sets. This may give your muscles further stimulation. But use drop sets sparingly as if not, within time, the muscle will become accustomed to them.

Printed in Great Britain
by Amazon